INTRODUCTION

This book is about one of the world's earliest and most advanced civilisations in the history of mankind. The Ancient Egyptian Empire was centred around the fertile Nile valley in North Africa, where surplus crops created great wealth for her rulers. It remained a great power in the Middle East for about 2,500 years.

The Ancient Egyptians had many things we think of as modern, such as clocks, anaesthetics, doctors, a police force and equal rights for men and women. They had hundreds of different gods and built some of the most famous landmarks in the world, including the pyramids and the Great Sphinx at Giza.

Their rulers have become well known to us through the discovery of their remains, such as the famous tomb of the boy king Tutankhamun.

You can learn about the fascinating story of the Ancient Egyptians and how a typical family lived through the eyes of a boy named Badru and his sister Anka, in the following pages of this book.

CONTENTS

Written & illustrated by William Webb
Front cover illustration by Les Ives
Published by Colour History Ltd © 2005
Print reference number 29658/04/08

ⳉ INTRODUCTION

Ancient Egypt grew from many small villages, each with their own chief or god. In about 3100 BC these villages merged to form the kingdoms of Upper Egypt with its symbol of the lotus flower and Lower Egypt, whose symbol was the papyrus plant.

Around 3100 BC King Menes, also known as Narmer of Upper Egypt, fought and conquered Lower Egypt and united the kingdoms for the first time. As well as founding a new capital city at Memphis, Menes combined the white crown of Upper Egypt and the red of Lower Egypt to create a new double crown.

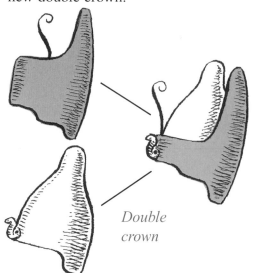

Double crown

The Great Sphinx at Giza

Historians have divided Ancient Egypt into different periods of time according to who ruled. The reigns of pharaohs, or kings, are grouped together into dynasties. These dynasties are then grouped together into 'periods' or 'kingdoms'.

The word **Pharaoh** comes from the Ancient Egyptian word for 'great house' (per-ao), or the palace where the King lived and it was a respectful way of referring to him. A pharaoh's wife was called the 'Great Royal Queen', but on rare occasions women ruled Egypt as pharaoh.

The Old Kingdom 2686 BC
One of the greatest periods in Egypt's history began in the 3rd dynasty. Because there were wise people ruling the country, Egypt became very wealthy by trading their goods with other countries. This is when many of the pyramids and the Great Sphinx were built.

The Middle Kingdom 2140 BC
After The Old Kingdom collapsed there was a period of civil war, but in 1991 BC Amenemhet, who was an official, seized the throne and went on to found the 12th dynasty. He helped Egypt to grow stronger, but because weak kings ruled for the next few dynasties, the Hyksos from Asia invaded and gained control of Egypt by 1674 BC.

The New Kingdom 1552 BC
The Hyksos were driven out and King Amosis conquered a vast empire. Royal tombs were built in the Valley of the Kings. Egypt reached the height of its power under King Tuthmosis, but was attacked by the Sea Peoples during the reign of Ramesses III. Even though Egypt defeated the Sea Peoples she was greatly weakened and slowly began to decline.

The Late Period
Egypt was ruled by foreign kings after the 20th dynasty and in 332 BC it was conquered by Alexander the Great. In 30 BC the last Egyptian monarch, Queen Cleopatra, committed suicide when the Romans attacked and took control of her country.

Mediterranean Sea
Alexandria
LOWER EGYPT
Bubastis
Heliopolis
Giza
Cairo
Saqqara
Memphis
River Nile
El-Amarna
UPPER EGYPT
Abydos
Karnak
Valley of the Kings
Thebes
Luxor
Aswan
NUBIA
Abu Simel

Writing

The Egyptians invented a type of writing using pictures called 'hieroglyphs'. It was used only on monuments, temples, tombs and religious scrolls. For business, letters and stories, they used a quick version of hieroglyphs called 'hieratic' script. They wrote from right to left on scrolls made of papyrus and this is where the word 'paper' comes from. They used reed pens and ink made from soot and water mixed together. An even faster way of writing using 'demotic' script came later. Towards the end of Ancient Egyptian civilisation the language of their conquerors, Greek, was used as well.

Hieroglyphs

The Rosetta Stone was discovered in Egypt in 1799 by one of Napoleon's soldiers. It had three pieces of text written one below the other. One of these texts was written in hieroglyphs, a language that had been forgotten for over a thousand years. In the 19th century French Egyptologist, Jean-Francois Champollion realised that the three pieces of text all said the same thing. He was able to decode the hieroglyphs at the top of the stone by reading the Greek text at the bottom. His discovery has allowed us to learn more than we could have hoped possible about life in Ancient Egypt.

Archaeologists have been able to learn many things about the Ancient Egyptians by studying the scenes and writing on papyri, paintings and mummies found in the tombs and temples they built. Other objects made by jewellers, potters, carpenters and metalworkers have been studied and displayed for us to see in museums around the world.

Can you work out what your name and address would have looked like in hieroglyphs?

The Rosetta Stone

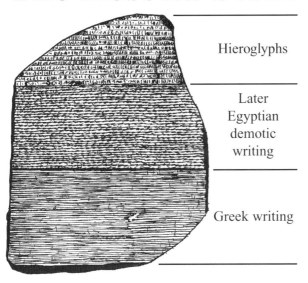

Hieroglyphs

Later Egyptian demotic writing

Greek writing

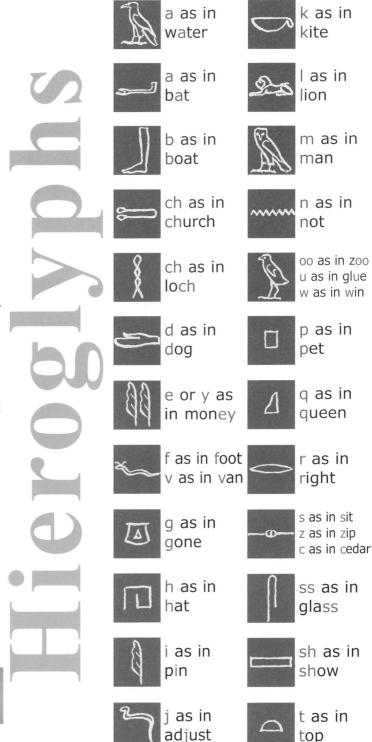

Symbol	Sound
	a as in water
	a as in bat
	b as in boat
	ch as in church
	ch as in loch
	d as in dog
	e or y as in money
	f as in foot / v as in van
	g as in gone
	h as in hat
	i as in pin
	j as in adjust
	k as in kite
	l as in lion
	m as in man
	n as in not
	oo as in zoo / u as in glue / w as in win
	p as in pet
	q as in queen
	r as in right
	s as in sit / z as in zip / c as in cedar
	ss as in glass
	sh as in show
	t as in top

Numbers

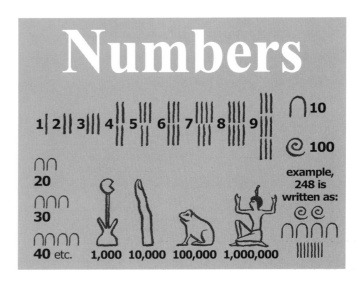

1 | 2 || 3 ||| 4 |||| 5 ||||| 6 |||||| 7 ||||||| 8 |||||||| 9 ||||||||| 10

20 / 30 / 40 etc.

100

1,000 / 10,000 / 100,000 / 1,000,000

example, 248 is written as:

⚖ TECHNOLOGY

The Ancient Egyptians were an extremely intelligent and skilled civilisation. Whilst people in Britain lived in simple dwellings, the Egyptians built beautiful temples and their artists painted wonderful scenes on the walls of their buildings, statues and on papyrus.

Astronomy

Astronomers made maps of the movements of the sun, moon and stars, which they used to create a calendar. They could predict when the Nile would flood. For example, the New Year started when Sirius, the 'dog star' appeared, which always happened just before the Nile waters rose. Their calendar had 365 days divided into 12 months of 30 days each, with 5 days of celebration at the start of each year. Because they had no leap year, their calendar was not as accurate as a modern calendar.

Egyptian Seasons
(based on the cycles of the Nile)

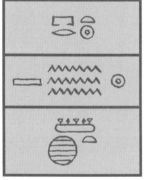	**Proyet** 'Emergence' Approx. Oct 21st - Feb 21st
	Shomu 'Summer' Approx. Feb 21st - June 21st
	Akhet 'Inundation' Approx. June 21st - Oct 21st

Measuring

Ancient Egyptians didn't use rulers to measure things, instead they used parts of their bodies. 1 cubit was equal to the length of an arm from the elbow to the end of the middle fingertip. A 'royal cubit' was a black granite rod approximately 52cm long that was used as a definite measure in times of confusion or disagreement.

Telling the Time

Clocks were invented using firstly the sun, but later water. Stone containers had a hole bored in them towards the base. The hole was filled with a bung made out of reeds, which let the water flow out slowly. People could tell the time by checking the level of the water against the marks inside. The clock was refilled every morning and was wider at the top to account for water pressure.

Architecture

The Ancient Egyptians had brilliant mathematicians who used their intelligence to design and build tombs and temples. Architects and engineers made such good calculations, that the angles at the corner of the base of the Great Pyramid were equal to within a fraction of a degree. Though they are the oldest and largest stone buildings in the world, the pyramids were so well built they still survive today.

Red Letter Days

Ancient Egyptians had a calendar of lucky and unlucky days. Lucky days were marked in black and unlucky days were marked in red. On the red days bad things had happened to their gods and they believed that if they did anything on these days it would end in disaster. The red colour reminded them of dry deserts.

Money

Money did not exist in Ancient Egypt until 305 BC. The value of goods was worked out according to their weight in copper. They were measured against a 'deben', originally around 14g of copper, which was later revalued at 91g and divided into 10 'kite'. Weights could be made out of metal or stone.

The Suez Canal

Around 600 BC the Egyptians started building a canal which would join the Mediterranean and Red Sea. This cut many miles and hours off the long journey by sea from Asia to Northern Europe. The Persians finished building the canal in about 500 BC, but it was filled in after being used for over a thousand years. The modern Suez Canal, which was finished in 1869 after a 16 year building programme, is witness to the skill and dedication of the early builders.

Medicine

The Egyptians were the first people to scientifically study the human body. They knew how to mend broken bones by setting them in splints or casts. Because of the mummification process they understood a lot about the heart and brain. They sterilised their instruments and knew about the importance of keeping the patient and his surroundings clean. They even had an anaesthetic and pain killer made from poppies, which are still used in painkillers today.

The US Navy aircraft carrier 'USS America' in the Suez Canal, 1990

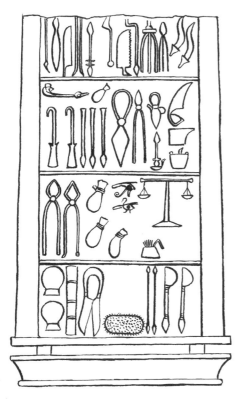

Ancient Egyptian medical kit

Medical cures taken from an Egyptian papyrus c1500-3000BC

Cure for Indigestion
Crush a hog's tooth and put it inside four sugar cakes. Eat for four days.

Cure for Diarrhea
1/8th cup figs and grapes, bread dough, pit corn, fresh earth, onion and elderberry.

Cure for Lesions of the Skin
After the scab has fallen off put on it scribe's excrement. Mix in fresh milk and apply as a poultice (a hot mixture used to ease irritation).

Cure for Cataracts
Mix brain-of-tortoise with honey. Place on the eye and say, "There is a shouting in the southern sky in darkness, there is an uproar in the northern sky, The Hall of Pillars falls into the waters. The crew of the sun god bent their oars so that the heads at his side fall into the water, who leads hither what he finds? I lead forth what I find. I lead forth your heads. I lift up your necks. I fasten what has been cut from you in its place. I lead you forth to drive away the god of Fevers and all possible deadly arts".

Can you create your own cure for an illness and draw the ingredients and tools you will need?

THE RIVER

"Hello, my name is Badru. I live in Egypt with my family on a farm which my grandfather has worked for many years. Our country is mostly desert. The only water we have, apart from an oasis here and there, comes from the River Nile.

"We need water for drinking and growing our crops. Because of the hot dry weather we have to water the crops regularly. To help us to do this we use a shaduf, which is a wooden frame with a bucket on one end and a weight on the other to help lift the water.

"It is the job of the ram-headed god Khnum to control the rise and fall of the water level. Too much or too little could mean the difference between us eating or starving. Everyone builds their home on high ground, so that they don't suffer flooding, but all the plants which need lots of water are grown near the banks of the River Nile, or beside the canals which lead from it. The Nile also gives us fish for eating, mud for bricks and pots and papyrus reeds to make boats, paper, shoes and other household things.

"There are three seasons in our year (see also page 5):

Ahket is when the river floods so we cannot work the land. This is when father and his friends sail to Memphis to work on the new buildings for King Tuthmosis. Everyone travels by boat because all of the towns and villages are close to the river.

Proyet is our sowing season when we plant barley and emmer wheat in the dark silt the floods leave behind. We call this rich fertile soil 'the black land'.

Shomu is when we harvest our crops".

The Nile god Hapi
Hapi was depicted as a bearded man with female breasts to represent fertility. He was very important to the Ancient Egyptians because he was the god of inundation who brought the flood each year. The flood deposited rich silt on the banks of the Nile, allowing the Egyptians to grow crops. He was helped by the god Khnum.

The ram-headed god Khnum

"Today I am going on my first hippopotamus hunt. I am nervous because these huge creatures can turn a small boat like ours over. At the front of the boat my brother has a harpoon to kill the hippo. They have asked me to steady the boat with a pole.

"I like being on the river. It's interesting to watch all the different boats travelling up and down. Apart from papyrus reed skiffs like this, there are also wide, flat-bottomed boats which we use to take our cows, ducks and grain to market in town. There are also huge wooden cargo ships bringing stone from the quarry at Aswan to use in the buildings at Memphis. There are pleasure boats taking people on cruises down the Nile and merchant ships either going to, or returning from, foreign ports across the seas. They will exchange Egyptian goods for things which we don't have, or we can't grow here.

Why was the river important to the Ancient Egyptians? Why did they need to travel to other countries?

"When we travel south we can use the north to south wind to fill our sails and help us to move more quickly. On the way back down the river we can travel with the current, using our oars to go faster. Last year the whole village came to the riverbank to watch a funeral barge make its way down river to the temple. It was a sad, but beautiful sight".

Nilometer
The Egyptians recorded the level of the Nile floodwater each year using nilometers. Nilometers were usually steps cut into stone which descended to the river. A scale was carved along the side of the steps from which the height of the river could be recorded. This was used to decide the amount of tax to be paid on the land.

BADRU'S HOUSE

"This is our house. It is built with bricks which are made by mixing Nile mud with straw and pebbles. As it is so hot we paint our houses white to reflect the heat of the sun. The small windows help keep out the heat and there is a vent on the roof to trap the cool north wind.

"I wish we had a pool like my uncle Neshi and his wealthy friends in town. It's full of lotus flowers and fish. He has planted palm and acacia trees around the edge, so that he can sit and relax in the shade while his servants cook, clean and do the gardening.

"My mother, Senen, is grinding the wheat to make dough for the bread which we eat every lunchtime with onions. The bread has bits of sand and grit in it which grinds our teeth down, but it tastes good and fills us when we are hungry. We cook our meals in a charcoal oven on the roof, because of the heat and smell.

"Paneb, my brother, is busy milking the cows, although I prefer drinking date or grape juice to milk. I am helping my father make beer. He makes it from mashed half-cooked loaves of barley bread mixed with water and sweetened with dates".

Making Beer

The bread and water ferment, then they are strained through a basket into jars, which are then sealed with clay. These are stored in a cool place, such as a cellar inside the house. The beer is drunk straight from the jar using a wooden straw with a filter because it is so lumpy.

Round loaves (see below) of bread are stuck on the outside of the oven and fall off when they are cooked. Wood was scarce, so they used vegetable waste and dung for fuel.

Father treads barley bread with water to make beer

A calf is tethered to the cow in order to encourage her milk production

A wooden straw

"My cat, Siti, is about to pounce on a bee. Cats are sacred and are protected by the goddess Bastet.

"Apart from the fish which my brother and I catch, we eat mostly beans, bread, onions, garlic and other vegetables and fruit. We only eat meat on feast days and for celebrations. My rich uncle eats ducks and geese. Grandfather built two beehives which provide us with honey for mother to use to make our favourite sweet bread for pudding.

Trailing plants are grown over a canopy to provide shade from the hot sun

Anka may have played with a wooden doll like this one, with beaded hair, or this could have been a temple offering

"My sister Anka's pet baboon, Ebo, is climbing the tree. He picks figs for us, which he drops into a basket made from papyrus leaves. Anka has become bored watching him and she is playing with her doll, which my uncle Neshi gave her for her birthday. She will be in trouble if mother sees her because we are expected to help around the farm".

Women

Women had the same legal rights as men. If their husbands treated them badly they could take them to court. The woman's main job was that of having and bringing up children. If she did not have a son, the husband could take a mistress to provide a male heir for the family. Women could be doctors, even priests, but they were mostly servants, weavers, basket makers, dancers, singers or musicians.

Badru's house looks very like the clay model of a house found in a Middle Kingdom tomb at Abydos, and now on display in the Kelvingrove Art Gallery and Museum in Glasgow. The ancient Egyptians believed that the soul or 'ka' of the deceased could live in the house and come out of its door into the walled yard to feast on the model offerings placed there. The 'soul-house' shows us what an Egyptian house looked like 4,000 years ago.

Bastet

Cats were very important to the ancient Egyptians. They had their own goddess called Bastet. She was first worshipped in Bubastis, but was later popular throughout Egypt and she was celebrated every year with a festival.

Can you guess what the objects below were used for?
(answers at the bottom of the page)

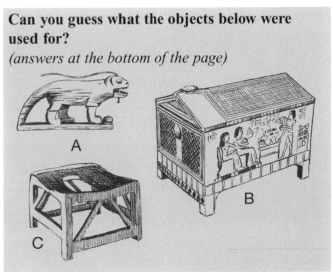

Answers to object quiz:
A Child's wooden toy.
B Linen chest belonging to a wealthy family.
C Lavatory seat which belonged to a foreman in charge of workers who built royal tombs. A clay pot filled with sand went under the seat and was emptied by servants.

10

FASHION

"Hello, my name is Anka. I am waiting for my big sister, Neema, to teach me how to spin and weave flax into linen cloth.

"We were supposed to start when the water in the clock reached the next level down, but she is late. I don't mind, it will give me a chance to look at all her beautiful things, like a kohl holder Uncle Neshi gave her when she was married last year. The wedding was wonderful. I had my hair beaded and patterns were painted on my hands and feet with henna, which stayed on for weeks. Mother sprinkled our clothes with sweet smelling perfume. Neema's dress was beautiful as it had hundreds of tiny pleats all drifting to the ground like water. She was wearing a black wig with a circlet of flowers and green eye make-up.

"Badru had his hair plaited. Like most boys he has only one small piece of hair on one side of his head. We call this the 'lock of youth'. Ti, Neema's husband, is a policeman. I was really frightened the first time I saw him in uniform, but now we get on really well and I love hearing his stories about the criminals he has caught. Last year a man was found guilty of robbing a tomb. I knew this was a very serious crime, but I was shocked to hear that the robber was punished by being impaled on sticks and left to die. What a slow and painful death.

"I wish Neema would hurry up now. Father needs the cloth for a new kilt. All our clothes are white to reflect the heat of the sun and help keep us cool. Young children often wear nothing at all. It is our father's job to clean all of our clothes, they have to be washed in the River Nile, which is full of crocodiles and very dangerous".

Jewellery
Everyone wore jewellery, whether it was beads for the poor, or gold if you were wealthy. They wore rings, ear studs, earrings and necklaces.

Women in Pharaoh's court would tie scented animal fat to their wigs, which would melt and slide down the wig

Tweezers to pluck unwanted hair

The Petrie Museum
The oldest surviving dress in the world can be found at the Petrie Museum of Egyptian Archaeology in London. The Tarkhan Dress, named after the location in Egypt where it was found, is a linen tunic which would have been worn by a child of about ten years old. It is dated at around 2,800 BC. The Petrie Museum have a large collection of beads and jewellery and cosmetic items, such as tweezers and mirrors.

Make-up
Everyone, including children, wore eye make-up. Green and black were the most popular colours. By the time of the New Kingdom, black, or 'kohl' had become the most popular. It was made from powdered galena, which was lead sulphide and protected the eyes from the glare of the sun and infection.

Wealthy People
Wealthy people wore clothes made of much finer linen than poorer people. They wore sandals made of leather, but the poor had shoes made of reeds. The women wore wigs, which were usually made from real hair. They decorated the wigs with jewelled tiaras.

⬙ TOWN LIFE

Badru is very excited today because he has come to town for the first time. His father has brought him along to help take the grain they owe to the priests, as tax for using their land.

"We are staying with Uncle Neshi in his villa. It is big and beautiful compared to our house. I am standing on the roof terrace looking down onto the quay. It is very noisy and busy with the smells wafting up from the food stalls below - it is making me feel hungry. Boats of all sizes jostle for space in the water. Small fishing skiffs like ours are weaving amongst the bigger ships.

"Everywhere people are busy loading and unloading goods, which they have brought to sell at the market. There are farmers like us exchanging cows, ducks and grain for food, clothes and furniture. Foreigners from Nubia, Palestine, Syria and Asia have brought things we do not have in Egypt, such as wood, incense, ebony, horses and even giraffe's tails.

"Father laughed at the look on my face when I saw an ostrich being unloaded from a southern boat. It is a gift for Pharaoh. After we have been to the temple we are going to an inn, where we will eat, drink beer, watch dancers and play Senet".

A landowner on a trip with his family

Boats travelling south used sails because the wind blows south, whilst boats going north, which is the direction of the current, used oars

A barge transporting obelisks being towed downstream

A fishing boat with a net full of fish

A barge carrying a large block of stone

The Police
By the time of the New Kingdom there were three types of police force:
The Medjay were made up of mercenaries from Nubia who guarded the royal tombs and protected the city of Thebes.
The Nuu helped local officials to oversee temple worship and patrolled the borders. Border police used trained dogs to track down criminals.
The Army were used to patrol remote areas.

Thieves were fined and beaten. Soldiers who ran away from the army were sent to the desert. Judges who tried to cheat the system could have their ears and noses cut off. There were prisons, but criminals were usually sent to work in labour camps, where they would be made to drag stones or dig canals. One of the worst punishments was to be sent to the Nubian gold mines, or turquoise mines in Sinai.

Senet was a board game which was played all over Egypt by people of every age. Unfortunately the rules have not survived, but we know it was played with counters and there were lucky and unlucky squares. They did not have dice until much later, so they threw marked sticks or bones.

THE TEMPLE

"We have arrived at the temple. It is the biggest and most beautiful building I have ever seen. Only priests are allowed inside, but ordinary people like us can go into the courtyard.

"There is a long queue of people waiting to buy offerings from the priest at the entrance. Most have bought cone-shaped loaves, but some have model scarab beetles and one has a mummified cat. They will place these things on the shrine in the courtyard wall as a gift to our god Amun-Re. It is the priest's job inside the temple to look after our god and keep him happy by offering prayers and food and by burning incense.

"Priests have to be very clean, so they wash at least four times a day and shave their heads and bodies to keep them free of hair. They teach young people how to become priests and to look after the temple gardens. There is a sacred pool, which holds the temple's holy water. There are also Houses of Life, which are offices and Houses of the Book, which are libraries.

"Priests never eat pork, as it reminds them of Set who is the evil god of chaos and confusion. Father's friend Tey is a scribe who learnt how to write at scribe school in the temple. He has lived and worked here ever since. Most people cannot read or write, but we can pay the scribe at the entrance and he will write out our wishes for us to offer to our god.

"Tey now looks after the craftsmen in the temple workshop. They make beautiful things out of wood, clay, glass and metal for the priests. He weighs valuable things like jewellery after they are made, to make sure that no one has stolen any gold".

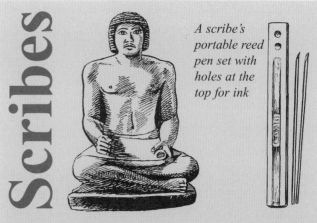

Scribes

A scribe's portable reed pen set with holes at the top for ink

Most people could not read or write. Scribes wrote and copied texts and kept records using 'hieratic' writing (see page 4). Records were very important to the Egyptians, so scribes enjoyed special privileges and power. Being a scribe was the first step to a good career in the government.

A mummified crocodile. When alive it was worshipped as the animal sacred to the god Sebek. You can see an example of a mummified crocodile in the Egypt Centre, Swansea.

If you visited a church today would you find any similarities between it and an Egyptian temple? Draw some things which are the same for Egyptian worshippers and for people worshipping God in a church today.

 # THE TEMPLE WORKSHOPS

"Tey, the scribe, told father that we can have a quick look around the temple workshops. We are lucky because people are not normally allowed inside, but it is busy, noisy and very hot in here.

"There are men working over open fires which seem to be burning everywhere. Some are melting metal to pour into moulds, others are dipping objects into liquid gold. To my right are kilns, used to fire the pottery which is being made on the potters' wheels. Beyond them craftsmen are making beautiful glass containers.

"As we walk on, I ask Tey what the terrible smell is. He explains that it is probably the alum, which is used to 'cure' animal skins so they can be made into leather. Can you see the stonemasons carving the huge lump of stone? They are following strict rules, which say how people should look. Once they have finished carving, they polish the stone with a rough powder and then artists will arrive to paint the sculpture.

"There is an old man teaching a young boy how to make a stool. We do not have much wood in Egypt, so carpenters have to be very good at using small pieces that can be joined together. I ask Tey if we can see the jewellers at work, but he cannot allow us because of the value of the gold and jewels. It's been a wonderful experience, but I am relieved to walk back outside into the fresh air again".

Education

Priests taught boys from families who could afford it. Discipline could be very harsh, with pupils being beaten. The very wealthy had private tutors at home. Girls learned skills like weaving from their mothers.

To Make Paper

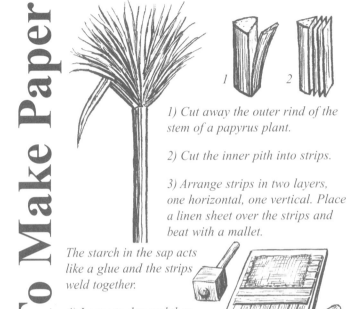

1) Cut away the outer rind of the stem of a papyrus plant.

2) Cut the inner pith into strips.

3) Arrange strips in two layers, one horizontal, one vertical. Place a linen sheet over the strips and beat with a mallet.

The starch in the sap acts like a glue and the strips weld together.

4) Leave to dry and then polish with a stone.

Gold was very carefully weighed and the precious stones used for jewellery were recorded so that nothing went missing.

GODS & GODDESSES

There are different myths which explain how Egypt was created, but they all agree that before the world began there was a watery darkness, which was ruled by the god Nun.

One myth, which goes back to the Old Kingdom, says that the sun god Atum created himself from Nun's dark world by magic. When Atum sneezed he made air, which was ruled by Shu, and moisture was ruled by the goddess Tefnut. Shu and Tefnut gave birth to Nut, goddess of heaven and Geb the god of earth. They fell in love and had two sons called Osiris and Set and two daughters called Isis and Nephthys.

Nut and Geb had brought heaven and earth together, so kings after them were thought of as living gods on earth. Osiris became the first pharaoh of Egypt and ruled happily with his half-sister Isis.

They were thought to have created and shaped the world, protecting it and helping good to overcome evil.

Egyptians believed that their country was the centre of the world, the point where everything had come into being. A new pharaoh would release four birds to the north, south, east and west to tell the entire world that a new reign had begun.

The Egyptians worshipped hundreds of different gods and goddesses, some of whom you have already read about in this book. Here are some of the more famous ones.

Amun-Re
Amun-Re was originally Re, Sun God and the King of Egypt and Amun, the local god of Thebes. When Thebes was made the capital city of Egypt, the two gods joined to become chief god and protector of pharaoh.

Osiris
Osiris was King of the underworld and the second most important god. He was the first to die and live again, which was the ambition of every Egyptian. When a pharaoh died, he became Osiris.

Isis
She was a devoted sister-wife of Osiris. Egyptian women looked up to her as a role model of a wife and mother. You can see a model of Isis with her son Horus at the Egypt Centre in Swansea.

Set
He was the god of trouble, evil and storms and Osiris's evil brother.

Horus
This god was the son of Osiris and Isis and he inherited his father's throne after Osiris died. All pharaohs became the living embodiment of Horus when they became king. He fought Set, his father's murderer, losing an eye in the battle. It was restored to him and his eye became a symbol of protection. He is often shown with a falcon's head.

Bes

Bes was a dwarf and a jester. He protected the house and family, especially children. Though he did not have a temple of his own, there were models of him in most homes, as he was very popular with ordinary Egyptians. He was the only god to be shown from the front, so he may have been adopted from another culture.

The Story of Osiris

The ancient Egyptians placed statues of gods and goddesses made of precious metals in their temples. At The Burrell Collection in Glasgow you can see a large bronze statue of the god Osiris from the Late Period. The Egyptians believed he was once the King of the living, but he was murdered by his ambitious brother Set. He was brought back to life through the love of his sister-wife, Isis, to rule again as the King of the dead. As a mummy his statue is wrapped in a shroud, but as a king he holds the crook and flail, which are symbols of kingship and he wears a long curved beard and elaborate crown.

Can you draw a picture of an imaginary god or goddess? What would you want them to help you protect and why?

Thoth

He is usually shown as a baboon, or ibis. As he was the god of wisdom and writing he was made the patron god of the scribes. Officials, mathematicians and engineers worshipped him as well. He was a moon god and a god of healing.

Ma'at

This goddess stood for truth, justice, order and the balance of the universe. She is usually seen wearing 'the feather of truth' on her head.

Ptah

The priests at Memphis believed that Ptah was the supreme god and that he created every other god by speaking their names. He was the god of craftsmen.

Nephthys

The goddess Nephthys helped her sister Isis to bring the mutilated body of Osiris back to life after he had been murdered by his brother Set. Together they protected coffins and canopic jars. They were often depicted as a pair of hawks.

Sobek

Sobek the crocodile god was seen as the ruler of water. The Nile was thought to be his sweat. Not surprisingly he was worshipped most in places where crocodile attacks were common.

PHARAOHS

The Kings of Egypt, or pharaohs, had absolute power over the whole country.

A pharaoh had many servants to attend to his every need. Officials helped him rule Egypt - two viziers ran Upper and Lower Egypt. Government officials were in charge of the treasury and royal works such as temples and tombs, the granaries, cattle and foreign affairs. After them came the high priests followed by mayors and governors who ran the towns and country districts. The King was head of the army, high priest of all the temples, he judged criminals and set the taxes.

The Ancient Egyptians believed that their King was the living embodiment of the god Horus. When he died he became Osiris, god of the underworld, achieving eternal life for himself and for his people. His successor, the new pharaoh, became Horus and took part in the burial of the old pharaoh who was now Osiris, just as the god Horus did for his murdered father Osiris. By taking part in the burial of a pharaoh, a person with no right to the throne could strengthen his claim to be the King of Egypt.

Pharaohs could have more than one wife, but the 'Great Royal Queen' was the most important. She was thought of as a god on earth because it was believed the goddesses Hathor and Isis blessed her. It was her eldest son who became heir to the throne, but if she could not produce a male child, then a son from another of the pharaoh's wives would inherit the title. Often the pharaoh married his sister, cousin, or even daughter in an attempt to try and keep the royal line pure.

The Army

If the country went to war, the pharaoh had to lead the army into battle. Officers helped him organise the soldiers who fought on foot, in chariots or by ship. Not all soldiers were volunteers. Scribes made lists of all the able-bodied young men, who the pharaoh could call on if he needed fresh conscripts in a time of war.

In the New Kingdom, the army was made up of three types of troops. The 'Braves' were elite troops like the SAS, who were trained for special missions. The 'Veterans' were men who were experienced at fighting and formed the front ranks in a battle. The 'Recruits' were volunteers, or conscripts who were not as experienced and were kept at the rear, or in reserve.

A lightly armed foot archer wearing a quilted headdress

Typical Egyptian fortifications

If a soldier had been brave and had done well in battle he was rewarded by the pharaoh, who presented him with a golden fly to be worn proudly around his neck

Padded linen cuirass

Wooden shield covered in cow hide

Spear

A 'khopesh' or sickle-shaped sword, or sometimes an axe. In earlier times, the soldiers fought wearing only a kilt and sometimes carrying an axe, or a mace.

The 'shenti' was a triangular piece of stiffened linen used to protect the soldier below the cuirass

Typical heavy-armed foot soldier of the New Kingdom

Hand Count
After a battle, soldiers would cut off the hands and other body parts of the enemy dead and put them into piles. Scribes would count the body parts and write down the number for the official records.

FAMOUS KINGS & QUEENS

OLD KINGDOM

Djoser

2667-2648 BC

Built the first 'step' pyramid at Saqqara where he was buried.

Khufu (Cheops)

2551-2528 BC

Built the Great Pyramid at Giza.

Khafra

2520-2494 BC

Built the second pyramid at Giza and the Great Sphinx which guards it. The face is possibly a portrait of the pharaoh.

NEW KINGDOM

Hatshepsut

1490 - 1468 BC

A rare female pharaoh.

Tuthmosis III

1506 - 1450 BC

After Hatshepsut's departure, he had all of her sculptures mutilated. A warrior king who conquered Syria and Palestine.

Amenhotep III

1402 - 1364 BC

Built the temple at Luxor and the Colossi of Memnon

Akhenaten

1364 - 1347 BC

Created a new city 'Akhetaten' at modern El-Amarna. He closed the temples of all the old gods and promoted the worship of the sun god Aten. His chief wife Nefertiti may have continued to rule after his death.

Tutankhamun

1347 - 1337 BC

The 'boy king'. He ruled for 9 years, but died at age 18 or 19. Famous because his tomb was discovered intact in the Valley of the Kings by Howard Carter in 1922.

Seti I

1303 - 1290 BC

A great warrior king who drove back the Hittites in Syria.

Ramesses II

1290 - 1224 BC

Fought with the Hittites who he claimed to defeat at the Battle of Qadesh. He reigned for 67 years and built more monuments and statues than any other pharaoh.

LATE PERIOD

Cleopatra VII

51 - 30 BC

Last Ptolemic ruler. She committed suicide when Octavian, later named Augustus, defeated her at the Battle of Actium.

The step pyramid at Saqqara as it would have looked in 2680 BC. It had one true entrance (on the left in this picture) and the other thirteen were false entrances.

Hatshepsut   **Tuthmosis III**

You can experience the magnificence and wonder of the world's greatest discovery of ancient treasure at the Tutankhamun Exhibition in Dorchester. You can explore the ante-chamber filled with treasures and enter the burial chamber to witness Howard Carter raising the golden coffins. In the Hall of Treasures you can see facsimiles of some of Tutankhamun's greatest golden treasures, including the famous golden funerary mask.

The Colossi of Memnon, huge seated statues of Amenhotep III, which were originally part of his temple at Thebes. They date from the 14th century BC.

DEATH & THE AFTERLIFE

"Today is a sad day for us. We have just been given the news that Uncle Neshi died two weeks ago. He was my father's brother.

"We are his only living relatives, which means that father will inherit his house. Uncle's funeral will take about 70 days to arrange. When he was alive, he hired a carpenter to make a model of the boat which will take him on the dangerous journey through Duat, the underworld. This dangerous place is full of monsters and here Anubis will weigh Uncle's heart to see if it is lighter, or heavier than 'the feather of truth'. If lighter, his spirit will be free to pass through to the 'Field of Reeds', but if it is heavier, his heart will be thrown to Ammit, the devourer of the dead, who will eat it and end his journey.

"Once he reaches his next life, Uncle will need somewhere to live, which is why he had a clay model of his house made. It is possible that Osiris, the ruler of the underworld, may want him to work in the fields in the next life. Several shabtis have been made, which are small wooden statues of labourers, who will do the work for him. He will also need clothes, food, cosmetics and jewellery, which will be placed in the tomb with him.

"I have seen the small brick pyramid which he built for himself. It has a passage leading to a burial chamber, where he will be placed with his possessions. Uncle will need his body in the afterlife, so it has to be preserved by the priests. The priest in charge of the burial wears the mask of Anubis, god of the dead".

Why Mummy?

The name 'mummy' dates from the 19th century AD. Arab discoverers thought the blackened skin of the mummies was because they were coated in 'mummiya', a kind of tar. It was actually the embalming resin which was black.

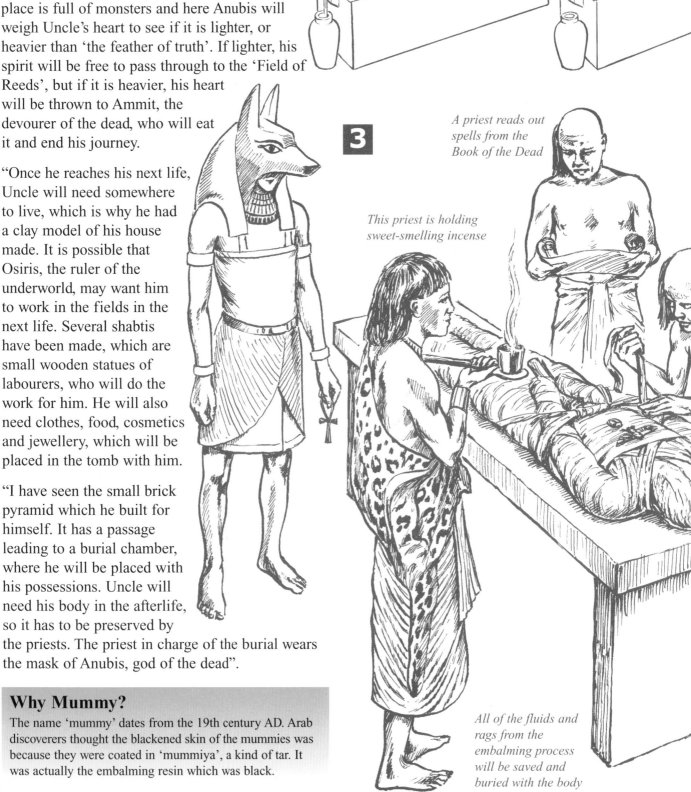

A priest reads out spells from the Book of the Dead

This priest is holding sweet-smelling incense

All of the fluids and rags from the embalming process will be saved and buried with the body

How to make a mummy

1 The body is washed with good-smelling palm wine and rinsed with Nile water.

2 A priest makes a cut in the left side and removes the organs. The body is then stuffed with natron, which is a kind of salt, to dry it out. After forty days it will be washed in Nile water and coated in oils to keep the skin elastic. The organs are wrapped in linen and put back in the body, which is packed with linen and sawdust so that it looks lifelike.

3 The body is then covered again in sweet-smelling oils and wrapped in linen. Fingers and toes are individually wrapped at the end. Amulets, such as an eye of Horus, or scarab beetles are put between the linen layers. Spells will be read out by a priest to ward off evil spirits and protect the body's journey to the underworld. A papyrus scroll with spells from the Book of the Dead is placed between the wrapped hands.

4 The body is continually wrapped, tied together and painted with resin. Finally, a large cloth is wrapped over the entire mummy. It is attached with strips of linen, which run from the top to the bottom of the mummy, and around the middle. By the Middle Kingdom, a painted mask made from linen strips coated in plaster was placed over the head and chest.

A ritual, the 'Opening of the Mouth', is performed to allow the deceased to eat and drink again. Now the body is ready for the journey to the afterlife.

5 The mummy was placed in a wooden coffin or stone sarcophagus as a home for the deceased to live in forever. The modern name 'sarcophagus' means 'flesh-eating', but it had the opposite effect by protecting the body from harm. At the Kelvingrove Art Gallery and Museum in Glasgow you can see the huge granite sarcophagus of Pabasa, a powerful official who worked for pharaoh Psamtek I at Thebes in the Late Period. It is carved to look like the mummy of Osiris, god of the dead, wrapped in a shroud held in place by bandages.

Canopic Jars

The internal organs of the deceased are removed, because they are the first things to decompose. By the time of the New Kingdom, the organs were placed in canopic jars packed with natron. Later they were put back into the body, but the tradition of having jars was kept.

Imsety **Hapy** **Duamutef** **Qebehsenuef**

Imsety the human-headed god looks after the liver.

Hapy the baboon-headed god looks after the lungs.

Duamutef the jackal-headed god looks after the stomach.

Qebehsenuef the falcon-headed god looks after the intestines.

Removing the Brains

The internal organs are washed and packed in natron to dry them out. The heart is left because it is considered to be the centre of intelligence and feeling. The brain, if it will not pour out easily, is removed with the aid of a long hook by pulling it out through the nostrils.

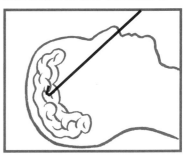

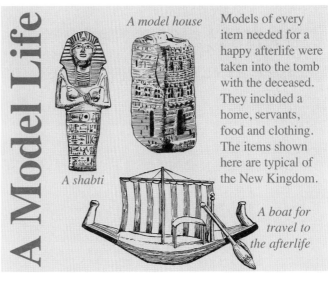

A model house

Models of every item needed for a happy afterlife were taken into the tomb with the deceased. They included a home, servants, food and clothing. The items shown here are typical of the New Kingdom.

A shabti

A boat for travel to the afterlife

You can come face to face with a recreation of Tutankhamun's mummified body at the Tutankhamun Exhibition in Dorchester. Here they have recreated his tomb, including treasures, using sight, sound and smell.

PYRAMIDS

The pyramids were built as tombs for dead pharaohs. There are over 80 in total, which are mostly ruined and half buried by sand. The earliest ones have stepped sides.

It is the pyramids of Giza, which were built more than 4,500 years ago for Khufu, Khafra and Menkaura, which are the largest and best preserved. The 'Great Pyramid' of Khufu was one of the seven wonders of the ancient world.

The Great Pyramid was positioned so that the four sides lined up exactly with true north, east, south and west. At the edge of the desert sits the Great Sphinx. This massive statue with its lion's body and king's head guards the royal pyramids of Giza. It is thought that the Great Sphinx's face was carved to look like the pharaoh Khafra.

Nobody is certain how the pyramids were built, but historians have estimated that it would have taken 20 years and 100,000 men to build the Great Pyramid at Giza. The centre of the structure was made from limestone, which could be quarried locally, but for the outer layer, limestone was brought in by boat from Tura, on the other side of the Nile.

When the pharaoh died his body was brought to the site in a funeral barge along the river. His coffin would have been carried along a causeway by mourners and placed in the mortuary temple. Priests would perform their sacred rites on the dead King, then they would lay him to rest in the burial chamber.

The Great Pyramid

The Great Pyramid was 146m tall and contained over 2.5 million blocks which were cut so precisely that the gaps between them are less than 0.5mm wide. The limestone casing made the pyramid gleam white in the sun.

How did they build the pyramids?

One suggestion is that the Egyptians used the shaduf (see page 7) to lift the stones to the next building level using workers as counterweights.

Another theory is that a huge ramp was constructed and the stones were dragged up the ramp on wooden sledges.

Wooden sledge

The workers who built the pyramids were not slaves, but free men who worked for a short time. They were fed, clothed and housed by the pharaoh and their tax bill was reduced. It was said that this pleased the gods.

Five chambers spread the weight of the stones above

Khufu's chamber

Grand gallery

Granite seal

Empty chambers

Escape shaft

Three pyramids where Khufu's chief wives were buried

Mortuary temple where offerings could be made

Desert bedrock

Height Comparison

Canary Wharf 235m

Great Pyramid 146m

Statue of Liberty 92m

Causeway to a temple at the edge of the Nile valley

Pit for boat to carry the pharaoh's body up the Nile